TALES OF THREE POPES

True stories from the lives of
Francis, John Paul II and John XXIII

Written and illustrated by
TED HARRISON

DARTON · LONGMAN + TODD

First published in 2014 by
Darton, Longman and Todd Ltd
1 Spencer Court
140 – 142 Wandsworth High Street
London SW18 4JJ

ISBN: 978-0-232-53108-4

A catalogue record for this book is available from the British Library.

Designed and produced by Judy Linard
Printed and bound by Scandbook AB

CONTENTS

TALES OF POPE FRANCIS

BIBLIOGRAPHY

INTRODUCTION

At the end of September 2013, Pope Francis announced that on 27 April the following year he would officially declare two of his predecessors Popes John XXIII and John Paul II to be saints.

The canonisation ceremony, the Vatican confirmed, would take place on the Sunday after Easter, the Feast of the Divine Mercy.

Such a ceremony is an acknowledgement that those being honoured as saints are people of exceptional holiness and virtue. Canonisation is the culmination of a long process during which the lives of those being canonised are scrutinised in detail and evidence is gathered that miracles have been performed which can be attributed to their intercession. In the case of Pope John a single miracle has been examined and confirmed. Many miracles have been attributed to Pope John Paul, although only two were required to be proven.

A canonisation is a major celebration. Thousands normally gather in St Peter's Square on the day, in a mood of joyful reverence. Never before have three popes been the simultaneous focus of attention in quite the same way; Popes John and John Paul as the new saints and Francis as the living pope publicly confirming their inclusion in the Church's calendar of honour.

Whatever direction the Roman Catholic Church takes in the future, it is highly likely that historians in years to come will consider these three popes, John XXIII, John Paul II and Francis to be the most influential and popular pontiffs of the modern era.

Angelo Roncalli, Pope John, who reigned for less than five years, called the Second Vatican Council and instigated an era of far-reaching change, especially in liturgy, enabling the words of the Mass to be accessible to all in their own languages. Karol Wotyla from Poland, Pope John Paul II, was the first non-Italian for many centuries to be elected pope, and became the most widely travelled in history. Jorge Bergoglio from Argentina, Pope Francis, in his first year of office has already set a radical and far-reaching agenda, refocusing the Church on its original purpose, to serve the poor and disadvantaged in society.

This book sketches portraits of the three men using stories from their lives that illustrate their respective characters. Many of the stories told about them have taken on the quality of legends. Some have no doubt been embellished with the retelling, but have not lost their essential truth for that.

The three popes came from three very different backgrounds. Pope John was born into a family of Italian peasant farmers. John Paul lived and worked under oppressive political regimes, first the Nazis and then the Polish puppets of the Soviet bloc. Pope Francis was brought up in the New World, in Argentina, a country of political tension and religious challenge.

Each man was elected to lead a worldwide Church and they brought three sets of remarkable and uniquely personal talents to the task.

JOHN XXIII:
Journal of a Soul

Angelo Roncalli kept a diary. He started writing it at the age of 14 and never let the habit lapse. One of the best-documented periods of his life was his time at the seminary at Bergamo where he was educated in preparation for ordination. In his very first entry he copied out a definition of what it means to be a 'model priest'. He also set out rules 'to be observed by young men who wish to make progress in the life of piety and study'.

He comes across as a serious, studious and scrupulous young man. If he had a weakness, it was a liking for good Italian food! To prevent his mind from straying into the territory of improper thought, the teenage Angelo confided in his diary that he would sleep 'with the Rosary of the Blessed Virgin around his neck' and his arms folded crosswise on his chest.

A recurring theme during more than 67 years as a diarist was his quest for holiness and his critical self-examination. He constantly set out what he ought to be aspiring to and measured himself against that ideal.

The diaries were never intended to be widely read, although they were later published as 'Journal of a Soul' and became a kind of autobiography. Because they were initially private meditations and reflections, what he wrote about himself was never tailored for any audience but his alone.

Even as pope he would remind himself in his diary of his pious duties. In 1961 he wrote, 'everyone calls me "Holy Father" and holy I must and will be'.

Angelo Roncalli was ordained deacon in 1903 and in that year wrote in his journal, 'God desires us to follow the examples of the saints by absorbing the vital sap of their virtues and turning it into our own life blood.'

At different stages through his ministry his self-examination would call for a refocusing of practice or devotion. 'Do your ordinary things day by day without ostentation,' he told himself at the age of 53. He was in his late sixties and apostolic nuncio in France, an important and dignified office, when he reminded himself to 'reduce everything, principles, aims, position, business to the utmost simplicity'.

An entry made when he was already in his seventies gives no indication that he had any thoughts that he might be pope. It modestly refers to 'the few years I have left'.

However Angelo Roncalli did become Pope John XXIII and far from being the safe caretaker pontiff many expected him to be, he called the historic Second Vatican Council. It was a visionary decision and involved a monumental task of organisation. Shortly before he died he was able to write, 'after three years of preparation, certainly laborious but also joyful and serene, we are now on the slopes of the sacred mountain'.

JOHN PAUL II:
Halina

The young man was destined for great things, of that his contemporaries were certain. Throughout his school days in Wadowice he had been academically head and shoulders above his classmates, as well as excelling on the sports field. Yet, reports from that time consistently attest Karol Wojtyla, or Lolek to his friends, was never boastful and always very popular.

When a bishop visited his school on one occasion, Lolek was appointed to offer a short speech of welcome on behalf of his fellow pupils. Afterwards the bishop said to his teacher, 'Is that boy going to become a priest?'

'It doesn't look like it at the moment,' came the reply.

'That's a pity,' the bishop said.

Karol as a student and young man was not someone of mere superficial brilliance. He had depth to his learning, derived perhaps from the sorrows in his life, in particular the early death of his mother and his older brother.

He wrote poetry and was a gifted stage actor. He later became a playwright. He was blessed with a fine physique, good looks and a commanding voice.

Those who knew Karol in his twenties might have guessed that he would make his name in the theatre. He was known to be a devout Catholic, but the priesthood? One day a bishop! Heavens no!

Indeed many thought at the time that Karol and his good friend Halina Krolikiewicz might one day marry. She was the daughter of his school's headmaster and they shared an interest in acting and the stage. During the Nazi occupation of Poland both were involved in the risky business of nurturing an underground theatre.

However strong his feelings towards her may have been, the call of the priesthood was stronger. Was there a moment when he broke the news to her that his future was not to be with her? Perhaps, it would have been a difficult emotional parting. Later, Halina was to marry a fellow actor and after the war Fr Karol baptised their daughter Monica.

On 16 October 1978 many of Karol's old friends from his days as an actor were watching the television for news from the conclave of cardinals meeting in Rome. As the words '*Habemus Papam*' were pronounced, one of them suddenly shrieked and started sobbing. She had spotted a familiar figure emerging from the shadows onto the balcony.

'What's the matter?' her husband asked.

'Jesus Maria,' she said between her sobs of joy and surprise. 'They've elected Lolek pope!'

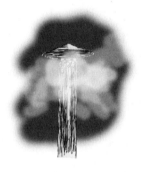

FRANCIS:
Vocation

The tango is Argentina's national dance. It can be danced in many ways. It can be rhythmic, athletic or erotic. As a teenager Jorge Bergoglio was good at the tango. Like many young men of his age he enjoyed dancing, football and the company of young women.

It is said that at the age of 17 he knew who he wished to marry and one September was due to join his girlfriend at his school's annual student picnic. He might even have had plans to propose to her.

On the morning of the picnic he was passing his local parish church and on the spur of the moment decided to go in and say a prayer. It was a perfectly normal thing for someone with his Church background and upbringing to do.

Inside he met a priest, Father Duarte, who he had not known before and the young man was immediately struck by his air of spirituality. He asked to make his confession.

Later Jorge Bergoglio was to recall how something strange happened to him during that interchange between him, the penitent, and the priest. 'It was to change my life. It was as if the priest had been waiting for me.'

Afterwards Jorge knew that he had to become a priest himself. He decided not to go to the student picnic and went home instead, his mind in a turmoil.

He completed his secondary and higher education, taking a diploma in chemistry, before, at the age of 21, breaking the news to his parents that he had a vocation to the priesthood. His father was pleased for him and his grandmother very supportive, but his mother reacted very differently. She had been led to believe her son was studying medicine. 'I am,' he reassured her, 'the medicine of the soul.' It was several years before she reconciled herself to the idea. Perhaps she felt that she was losing her son to the Church, or needed time to become accustomed to the idea.

Two events nearly diverted Jorge from his chosen path. He met a young woman at a family wedding and was immediately attracted to her. On returning to the seminary he found it hard to focus on his prayers, images of the young woman kept entering his head. It caused him to reconsider his vocation. After much heart-searching, he decided to remain true to his vocation, while acknowledging that such distractions were to be expected, they were normal distractions for a man choosing the path of celibacy.

The second event was of a very different kind. He

developed pneumonia caused by cysts on his lung. He needed to undergo emergency surgery and had part of his lung removed. Reflecting on his close encounter with death he saw the experience as one that put his life into perspective. Despite the severe pain, the illness confirmed his resolve to become a priest. A nun and family friend who visited him in hospital said something to him that struck a chord. 'You have been called to imitate Christ', she said. 'Suffering is not a virtue', he later wrote, 'but the way we encounter suffering can be virtuous'.

JOHN XXIII:
Padre Roncalli

Angelo Roncalli was nineteen when he took the train to Rome to become a student at the seminary in Piazza Sant'Appollinare. He had a room to himself furnished with the bare necessities. Angelo was an able student and quickly absorbed the rudiments of Catholic theology. He developed a special interest in history and won a prize for a paper in Hebrew.

Roman life was exciting. He was in the congregation at the Vatican when ten new cardinals were created and much enjoyed the splendour of the liturgy. He received a blessing from the 90 year-old Pope Leo XIII.

He and his fellow students were able, when not studying, to walk around the city in their purple cassocks. They saw the main archaeological sites and attended performances of approved sacred music. The country boy had his eyes opened. After one meeting with overseas priests at a missionary college he wrote in a letter to his family reporting that 'some of them had hands and faces as black as coal!'

He lived a frugal life of study and prayer. His clothes were all second-hand and the bursar would roam the refectory during meals urging the students, including Roncalli, to 'eat less'.

This fulfilling period of Angelo Roncalli's life was to come to an abrupt end after less than a year.

On the last day of November 1901 he was ordered back to Bergamo to join the army. He was to spent 12 months as a conscript and hated it. He called it his year of Babylonian captivity.

The physical training and harsh living conditions were not what troubled Private Roncalli, but the coarseness and barbarity of his fellow soldiers. As a future priest he was afforded some respect, but Angelo was quite unaccustomed to the bawdy barrack room banter that went on in his hearing. Seminary life was no preparation for the lurid language to which he had to listen.

When his time in the army was over he returned to Rome to continue with his studies, glad to exchange military for spiritual discipline.

Yet it was not the end of his army service. During the First World War he was called up again. This time, as a priest, he became an army chaplain. His opinion of his fellow soldiers was by then far more charitable and tolerant. He became a much loved and respected pastor, working in a military hospital. His main military fault was his lack of dress sense and he was reprimanded for the slovenly way he wore his uniform. He did however, in the fashion of the period, sport a rather splendid moustache.

No one doubted his courage. On one occasion a colonel was appointed who had strong anti-clerical opinions. He decided that all hospital orderlies, including priests, would have to strip and, like the other ranks, be inspected for signs of venereal disease. It was an order designed deliberately to humiliate the priests. Roncalli faced him down. Risking military punishment, he defied the order, saluted the colonel and marched out of the room. No further action was taken.

JOHN PAUL II:
The War Years

In September 1939, Germany invaded Karol Wojtyla's homeland from the west and Russian troops grabbed land to the east. Hitler's declared ambition, with Stalin's connivance, was to make Poland 'a long-forgotten name on an ancient map'.

Jews were to be exterminated, intellectuals removed and the Polish people forced into slave labour. As far as the Church was concerned Hitler had one role in mind, 'the task of a priest is to keep the Poles quiet, stupid and dull-witted'

For a devout Catholic, brimming with ideas, intellectual curiosity and ambition, the future looked very grim.

The war years were dangerous times. The 19-year-old student was determined to continue with his studies and became involved in the underground university movement. He helped found a secret theatre dedicated to Polish language drama. When he could, he helped Jewish families find new identities and escape the extermination camps.

To survive he had to be cunning and inconspicuous. If his papers were checked, he was seen to be a labourer. He had jobs at a stone quarry and later a chemical factory. It was hard manual graft, but Karol made many friends amongst his fellow workers. He was both a natural leader and a resourceful organiser and improvised classes and lectures to keep the minds of his fellow workers alive.

He took risks and knew that at any time he might be singled out by the occupying power as a troublemaker. Many of his friends 'disappeared'.

No one doubted his outer courage, but it masked an inner struggle. He felt, amidst the horror and danger, a strong call to the priesthood. Following the death of his father, a friend helped him discover the mystical writings of St John of the Cross. Following a serious street accident, Karol had time to consider his future. He knew ordination would change forever his relationship with his close friend Halina, an actress with whom he often appeared on stage. It would mean he would never have children of his own. It would mean dedicating his life entirely to God, to Mary and the service of others and all within a climate of political hostility to his vocation.

As he lay in his hospital bed, he weighed the options.

Karol Wojtyla prepared for the priesthood as a member of a semi-clandestine seminary and on All Saints' Day, 1946, he was ordained. His first mass, usually a joyous affair celebrated by the new priest in front of his family, was a sad affair. In the crypt of Wawel Cathedral he dedicated the mass to his family, father, mother and brother – all now dead.

JOHN XXIII:
Representing the Vatican

In 1925 Mgr Roncalli was appointed apostolic visitor to Bulgaria, and for ten years the future pope represented the Vatican in one of the Church's most demanding diplomatic posts.

Cardinal Gasparri, the Secretary of State, briefed him before he left. 'The situation is very confused. I can't tell you in detail what's going on. Everyone seems to be fighting with everyone else: Moslems with Orthodox, Greek Catholics with the Latins and the Latins with each other. Go there and find out what's really happening.'

For the next ten years Angelo Roncalli faced a thankless task. He set up home in Sofia and two of his unmarried sisters came with him to keep house and, when not entertaining, cook good Italian food.

Such were the tensions between the Christian Churches that when the 1600th anniversary of the Council of Nicea was marked, the official Orthodox

Church did not invite Rome's senior representative to any of the services of celebrations.

Eventually, by way of compromise, an event was organised in a mutually acceptable secular venue and Archbishop Roncalli was able to attend.

The Italian archbishop worked hard in his post to understand the local situation and keep lines of communication open with all sides. In time he came to speak Bulgarian fluently. His relations with Rome, however, were frequently strained and came to a head with the marriage of Bulgaria's King Boris III and Giovanna, the daughter of Italy's King Victor Emmanuel. It was a political match fraught with ecclesiastical difficulties.

Since King Boris was Orthodox and Princess Giovanna Catholic, a special dispensation had to be given by Pope Pius XI to allow the wedding to take place. Pius XI believed that the couple had agreed to raise the children as Catholics.

However when the firstborn, Princess Marie Luisa, was baptised by the Orthodox Metropolitan, the pope was not best pleased, to put it mildly.

Archbishop Roncalli was expected to write a stern letter of rebuke to the couple. He wrote more in sorrow than anger, but for his pains he was banished from court for a year. Yet he did not blame the queen personally and invited her to attend mass privately with him and shared some avuncular wisdom.

The King stressed that his decision had not been a snub to the pope, but he had acted out of concern 'for the interests of his torn and divided country'. The Communists seize upon anything that can turn the people against me', he claimed.

After the Orthodox baptism of the infant Prince Simeon, the story is told of how Archbishop Roncalli had to report back to the pope in person. Pius XI kept the portly 53 year-old kneeling in front of him for 45 minutes as a penance.

FRANCIS:
The Jesuits

When Jorge Bergoglio acknowledged his vocation to the priesthood, he went one step further and opted to join The Society of Jesus. He was to become one of 1200 Jesuits in South America, a member of a highly disciplined religious order founded in the sixteenth century by St Ignatius Loyola.

The Jesuit training is long and rigorous. Jorge Bergoglio began 15 years of study and preparation as a novice in 1958. His studies and preparation initially took him to Chile before he returned to Argentina to Santa Fe and Buenos Aires, both studying and teaching.

The Spiritual Exercises of St Ignatius are at the heart of Jesuit spirituality. They are designed to enable someone to discover a personal relationship with God through a structured and intense programme of silence, meditation and prayer lasting 30 days.

Jorge Bergoglio is known to have undertaken the

full 30 days of reflection at least twice and to have guided many others on their journey.

He took his perpetual vows in 1973, at the age of 36, by which time he was already a priest, and within three months was appointed Provincial Superior.

He became leader of an unhappy organisation. It would not be an exaggeration to say the order in his home country was in turmoil. The Society of Jesus in Argentina was losing members. Vocations had slumped. There were religious and political divisions. The more conservatively-inclined Catholics were worried that changes initiated by the Vatican Council were moving too fast. On the other hand there were Jesuits who had enthusiastically embraced Liberation Theology and moved into the slum areas to live alongside the most disadvantaged in an unequal society. Some in Rome viewed such gestures with suspicion and took Liberation Theology to be Marxism under a religious guise.

But whatever the political and theological tensions within the organisation, what all Jesuits had in common was their spiritual discipline and practice. As well as having undertaken the intense soul-searching of the Spiritual Exercises, Jesuits have a five-stage technique they use every day to reflect on God's purpose for them.

Every day a Jesuit gives himself time to become aware of God's presence; to review the previous 24 hours with gratitude in the company of the Holy Spirit; to reflect on the feelings and emotions experienced during the day; to select one particular feature of the day and examine it in prayer; to anticipate and prepare for the next day.

Like all Jesuits, Pope Francis knows and may often use the prayer of St Ignatius, 'Take, O Lord, and receive my entire liberty, my memory, my understanding and my whole will. All that I am and all that I possess you have given me: I surrender it all to you to be disposed of according to your will. Give me only your love and your grace; with these I will be rich enough, and will desire nothing more.'

JOHN PAUL II:
The Russian Soldier

With the end of the Second World War, Poland exchanged occupation by the German Nazis for domination by the Soviet Communists. Having narrowly escaped arrest, imprisonment and possibly death, at the hands of the Germans, in 1945 Karol Wojtyla came close to being arrested by the Russians. It was when he and a group of fellow students defiantly gathered in a Cracow market to sing patriotic and freedom songs.

Being warned of approaching danger, the students managed to disperse in the nick of time as the troops and police arrived.

So when one day a young Russian soldier arrived at the seminary where Karol Wojtyla was completing his preparations for ordination, he was naturally very wary.

Karol Wojtyla was taking his turn as porter and door-keeper when the bell rang.

'What do you want?' Karol asked the man standing on the doorstep.

'I wish to join the seminary,' came the totally unexpected reply.

In was an astonishing request. Was it a trick? It was all highly suspicious. Despite his reservations, Karol Wojtyla did not want to lose an opportunity to share his faith. After all it might have been 'heaven sent'.

The soldier was invited in and the two men talked at length. In the event the young Russian did not join the seminary, but the future pope later recalled their conversation as one that shaped his own thinking. The man had been brought up under a regime and in a society that specifically excluded and denounced God. He had hardly ever been inside a church. He knew nothing of theology or Church teaching. And yet, the man said, as he was being told there was no God, he knew instinctively there was.

Karol Wojtyla was deeply impressed and realised that even in the most discouraging circumstances, no one who truly wants to find God can ever be separated from him.

JOHN XXIII:
Islam and Secularism

By the time Archbishop Roncalli arrived in Constantinople, its new name of Istanbul was well established. With the Ottoman era having been consigned to history, by 1935, the city and the Turkish nation were part of a determinedly secular state. Under Ataturk, outward signs of religious commitment were discouraged. The popular fez was banned. At one time it had been worn by almost every Turkish man, but was now seen as a backward Islamic symbol.

To appear consistent, Christians were also told not to wear their distinctive clothing. Members of religious orders could not wear their habits and even the Vatican's representative had to dress in civvies. 'It's a great trial for everyone,' the archbishop wrote to a friend, but he also declared, 'What does it matter whether we wear a cassock or trousers as long as we proclaim the Word of God?'

The archbishop in sober suit and bowler hat was

described, a touch unkindly perhaps, as looking like a Lombardy businessman who found it difficult to cut down on the pasta.

A far more serious issue was protecting the Church's religious schools, a number of which were forced to close. As an apostolic delegate with no official diplomatic status, he had no effective government channels through which to protest.

The post to which Archbishop Roncalli was appointed included responsibility for the minority Roman Catholic communities in both Turkey and Greece. Relations with the Orthodox Church were as difficult as those with the secularist post-Islamic state and the posting was a major challenge calling on all the future pope's gifts.

On a personal front, his time in Turkey was not easy. News reaching him from Italy was often depressing. Mussolini was at the height of his powers and imperial ambitions. During that time too he heard of the death of his father and then of his mother.

His work focus was primarily pastoral. The story is told of a visit he made one evening to a small Latin church in Istanbul. He heard the congregation reciting prayers in French, the language commonly used in educated and intellectual circles in the region.

'Are the people here French?' he asked.

'No,' came the reply, 'they are Turkish.'

'Would it not be better for them to have a Turkish translation?'

Archbishop Roncalli arranged for a translation to be made and the following Sunday the members of the congregation found printed copies in the pews. It was an imaginative and welcome gesture at a time of heightened Turkish nationalism and, in a small way, a foretaste of the changes that Pope John's Vatican Council would in due course initiate, allowing Catholic congregations the opportunity to worship in their own languages.

JOHN PAUL II:
An Encounter with Padre Pio

On 16 June 2002 a crowd of 300,000 filled to overflowing St Peter's Square in Rome. The occasion was the canonization of Italy's most popular folk-saint of the twentieth century, Padre Pio. The saintly friar from San Giovanni Rotondo had not only been a much sought after confessor, he had also for much of his life carried the wounds of Christ, the stigmata, on his body.

After due consideration of his life, and the miracles attributed to him, Pope John Paul II declared Padre Pio a saint

Fifty-five years earlier Fr Karol Wojtyla, while

studying in Rome, went on pilgrimage to several of Italy's famous shrines and holy places. On his itinerary was a living shrine, the legendary Padre Pio. Fr Wojtyla attended mass at the friary at San Giovanni Rotondo in Foggia, Southern Italy, and made his confession to the friar. At that time, since travel was difficult, there were no great crowds clamouring for the future saint's attention and the young priest was able to spend some time with his confessor.

What transpired between the two will never be known, but many stories have been told since. One of the most persistent is that Padre Pio told the young Pole that he would one day 'gain the highest post in the Church.' When later he was appointed Cardinal, Karol Wojtyla believed the friar's prophecy had come true, not realising that its fulfillment was yet to come.

Another story tells of how the two priests entered into deep spiritual dialogue and the younger asked the older which of the wounds of Christ that he carried caused him the greatest suffering. 'It is my shoulder,' the friar confided, speaking of an invisible wound about which he had never previously spoken. In the Passion story Jesus carried his own cross that rested heavily on his beaten body.

Several years later a friend of Karol Wojtyla, Dr Wanda Poltawaska, was diagnosed with terminal cancer. By then a bishop, he wrote to Padre Pio asking for his prayers. Shortly before Wanda was due to undergo surgery for the removal of a tumour she was X-rayed by her doctor. Astonishingly the tumour had vanished. Bishop Wojtyla was convinced that a miracle had occurred.

Today many visitors to San Giovanni Rotondo say the prayer of Pope John Paul II to Saint Pio of Pietrelcina. It begins, 'Padre Pio, teach us also, we pray, humility of heart' and ends with the words, 'Accompany us on our earthly pilgrimage toward the blessed Homeland, where we too, hope to arrive to contemplate forever the Glory of the Father, the Son, and the Holy Spirit.'

JOHN XXIII:
Paris

Shortly after the liberation of Paris in 1944, Angelo Roncalli heard that he was to be transferred from Turkey to become the Holy See's representative in Paris.

Two days after Christmas he set out from Ankara and by a series of hazardous short-hop flights, via Beirut and Cairo, arrived in Rome. From there he was taken by French government plane to Paris. Initially all he could see of the city from the air was the Eiffel Tower emerging from a sea of mist.

On arrival he first visited the foreign minister, and then called to see Cardinal Suhard. Soon after he met with General de Gaulle.

Following the war years there was much call on the nuncio's diplomatic and pastoral gifts to heal the political, social and ecclesiastical wounds that had resulted from the German occupation.

Archbishop Roncalli endeared himself to the

people of France with his humour and simple manner. Once addressing a congregation the microphone system broke down. It was not restored until the end of his address. 'I can assure you,' the nuncio said to much laughter, 'you haven't missed much. It was a dull address and I don't speak French very well. I should have paid more attention to my lessons when I was young!'

He did in fact speak French well enough to be able to chat with everyone he met, although his accent and grammar were occasionally idiosyncratic.

He became a familiar figure in French society, accepting invitations and returning hospitality. His dining table became famous for its simple excellence. He distrusted the slick sophistication of modern French philosophy, both theological and secular, and preferred his conversations with ordinary Parisians. He would be seen out walking in the streets with a stick in hand stopping from time to time to pass the time of day with street vendors and shop keepers.

One-time French Prime Minister, Robert Schuman said of him, 'He is the only man in the whole of Paris who carries peace wherever he goes. As soon as you are near him, you can breathe it. Indeed you can almost touch it.'

JOHN PAUL II:
The New Overcoat

The young curate arrived at his new parish, St Florian's in Cracow, not in a taxi as expected, but hitching a ride on an old horse-drawn cart. Father Karol Wojtyla had nothing with him bar the under-clothes and cassock he was wearing, the black soup-plate hat on his head and a small case in his hand.

'Where is your luggage?' he was asked. 'I've got it all here,' he replied, pointing to the case.

Father Wojtyla had no interest in either possessions or appearances and the parishioners at St Florian's began to worry that as the cold Polish winter set in, his threadbare cassock would do little to keep him warm.

They offered to buy him a new cassock and an overcoat to go with it, but he politely declined the offer.

As the winter deepened Father Wojtyla spent hours tramping the streets visiting families. He sat for long periods in a draughty confessional. He would catch his death of cold, worried the women of the parish.

Eventually they went to the parish priest with their concerns. He, equally anxious that his curate might fall ill, ordered the young priest to accept the offer of a new cassock.

So, Father Karol agreed and thanked the parishioners for their kindness.

Yet there was still the matter of the overcoat. A group of parishioners bought some good thick material and tricked Father Karol into paying a visit to the tailor's house. Once there, and before the priest could protest, out came the tape-measure and Father Karol's measurements were taken. He had been well and truly ambushed.

When the overcoat was finished Father Karol expressed his sincere gratitude.

Over the next weeks, the churchgoers waited to see him wear it. He wore his new cassock regularly, but even on the coldest of days, he was never seen in his new coat.

Months went past and eventually the parish concluded Father Karol must have given his new overcoat away. He had probably met someone in greater need than himself and handed it over. A typically selfless gesture from a remarkable and highly unusual young man.

FRANCIS:
The Dirty War

Between 1976 and 1983 the Argentinian government waged what has become known as the Dirty War against suspected dissidents and subversives. Opponents of the military junta simply 'disappeared'. They were frequently taken to secret government detention centres, tortured and killed. It has been estimated that around 30,000 people lost their lives.

During the first years of this reign of terror Father Jorge Bergoglio was the provincial of the Jesuits in the country and responsible for the order's priests, several of whom bravely stood up to the regime.

Many people however thought that the Church was too non-critical, and in some instances gave implicit encouragement to the government. Father Bergoglio did not speak out, but to do so would have been to volunteer for martyrdom. Behind the scenes he was, however, actively involved in smuggling those in danger out of the country.

At the time he had a reputation as a conservative and as provincial found himself in conflict with two active supporters of Liberation Theology, Fathers Orlando Yorio and Francisco Jalics.

Angered by their disobedience he expelled them from the order and informed the archbishop, who withdrew their licences to celebrate public Mass. To the military regime this was a clear message, that the two men were no longer under the protection of the Church.

The two men were kidnapped one Sunday and for five days they were tortured in an attempt to get them to confess to being supporters of the regime's left-wing guerilla opponents. What made matters even worse for the two priests was that they believed that their provincial had betrayed them.

The future pope had not intended this, but realised their suffering was a direct consequence of his hasty and public disciplining of the two priests. They were held for five months, during which time their superior lobbied hard for their release. Eventually they were set free and allowed to leave the country.

After the overthrow of the regime, and by then an archbishop, and cardinal, Jorge Bergoglio talked of his mistakes. 'I made hundreds of errors, errors and sins. I ask forgiveness for the sins and offences I did indeed commit.'

A deep searching of his conscience brought about

a remarkable change. Once a political conservative, today Pope Francis is a champion of society's most disadvantaged.

When he was called upon to accept his election as pope, instead of simply saying the words, 'I accept' he replied, 'I am a great sinner, trusting in the patience and mercy of God in suffering, I accept.'

Father Jalics outlived Father Yorio and the day came when he had a chance to meet with his former provincial. After a long discussion they celebrated mass together and both were seen in tears as they embraced.

'What matters isn't Bergoglio and his past,' said the liberation theologian Leonardo Boff, 'but Francis and his future.'

JOHN XXIII:
Politics

The main political fault line in the industrial cities of Italy after the Second World War was between Catholicism and Communism; in black and white terms, Rome versus Moscow. Politics was passionate and divisive; elections were fiercely contested. In 1937 the Church had declared Communism to be intrinsically evil. The country's Christian Democrats had the tacit backing of the Vatican and were opposed by several Socialist and left-wing parties.

As Apostolic Nuncio in Paris in the immediate postwar years, Angelo Roncalli was drawn into a debate that much concerned the Curia in Rome. A number of priests felt that the Church should be siding with the poor and thus be far less politically right wing. They proposed leaving parish ministry, getting ordinary jobs and becoming worker-priests.

Many traditional, middle-class French Catholics complained to the nuncio that these priests were

Communists in all but name. They looked to Eastern Europe and saw how the Church struggled under Soviet Communism.

Guidance to the nuncio on what line to take was confused. Some Vatican officials were vigorously opposed to the worker-priest experiment. Others appreciated that the Church had to explore radical new ways of evangelising. In France barely 1% of working men attended Mass regularly.

When one left-wing French priest attended a meeting in Poland and was reported to have said that in the struggle for peace and justice 'we are all Communists', the French Cardinal Suhard issued a solemn statement denouncing collaboration with the political left.

The nuncio was careful never to show exactly where his sympathies lay. Was he with the hard-line anti-Communists or the radical priests who wished to work alongside the poor and disadvantaged?

The future pope's next appointment was to Venice as Patriarch and Cardinal. When, in 1957, the Italian Socialist Party chose the city as venue for its annual congress, Cardinal Roncalli could not ignore such a major event. In a Candlemas address he said that he welcomed the delegates, as St Paul had instructed a bishop to be hospitable.

And he went further than he had allowed himself to go in Paris. He spoke of a gap that had opened up between Christian and secular culture and prayed that the congress might help bridge this gap.

Vatican conservatives grumbled that the aging patriarch was too naïve and soft-hearted. But the cardinal received much public and private support for taking a wise and conciliatory position.

JOHN PAUL II:
The Mountains

When time permitted Father Karol Wojtyla grabbed every opportunity to leave city life behind and head for the countryside. In summer he looked forward to taking groups of his students from Lublin University to go hiking and kayaking in the mountains. In winter they skied. He found the rigours of outdoor life the perfect antidote to urban living and the strains of working under an authoritarian political system that was little more than a puppet of the neighbouring Soviet empire.

In the summer of 1958 he was enjoying the lakes of Mazuria in the north-east of Poland when a message reached him that he had to go to Warsaw for a meeting with Cardinal Wyszynski. There he discovered that, although he was only 38, The Vatican had approved his appointment as Bishop of Krakow.

'Am I not too young to be a bishop?' he queried.

'That,' replied the cardinal, 'is a weakness of which we are quickly cured.'

Karol Wojtyla was consecrated bishop on 28 September, exactly a month before John XXIII became pope.

Becoming a bishop involved several major changes in Karol's life. What saddened him most was that as Bishop Wojtyla he would no longer have regular contact with the students he so enjoyed teaching. He had been a highly popular teacher; they nicknamed him 'Uncle' and he loved the exchange of ideas with young and enthusiastic minds.

But some things did not change. He carried on living simply, riding his bicycle to appointments and his housekeeper despaired of the new bishop's lack of interest in his clothing and appearance.

For recreation he continued to head for the outdoors. He had much enjoyed leading student parties, but also cherished solitude. Away from his diocesan duties few would recognise him in his baggy trousers, hiking boots and woolly cap.

One day walking in the Tatra Mountains he paused to pass the time of day with a local shepherd and they shared some bread and sausage. They conversed in the local patois about this and that.

'And what do you do for a living?' the shepherd asked.

'I'm a bishop,' Karol Wojtyla replied, still in local dialect.

The shepherd roared with laughter. 'That's a good joke,' he said. 'If you're a bishop, I'm the pope!'

JOHN XXIII:
The Prison Visitor

When Pius XII died in 1958, he had been pope for almost 20 years. His papal style was firmly established at The Vatican.

But everything changed with the accession of the 77-year-old cardinal from Venice, Angelo Giuseppe Roncalli. It was, said one insider, as if the windows of the Vatican had been flung open.

The new pope, John XXIII, had a totally different manner. He was jovial and informal and little bothered by protocol. As one cardinal later observed, an audience with Pope Pius had been like undergoing a stiff oral examination, one with Pope John was like chatting with a favourite grandfather.

Yet his affability masked a highly disciplined and visionary mind. He tightened up the administrative machine and set in motion his ambitious plans to summons a Second Vatican Council.

First and foremost he saw himself as a pastoral pope. Not only was he the spiritual leader of the worldwide Church, he was also the Bishop of Rome. On the first Christmas of his pontificate he visited the city's Bambino Gesù Children's Hospital. The day after that he went to the Regina Coeli Prison. He embraced a murderer who asked him if he could ever be forgiven. Many of the inmates, in their striped prison uniforms, knelt to be blessed. He called them 'his sons' and joked with some that his own cousin, had been imprisoned in the same jail after being caught poaching. When he promised to remember all of them, as well as their wives and sisters, in his nightly rosary prayers, the prisoners applauded.

One of the prison chaplains said that the pope's visit was the most beautiful day of his life. Pope John confided in his diary that it was 'a simple and natural thing' to do.

He confessed that it took him a while to adjust to being pope and how awkward it felt to be addressed as 'Your Holiness' or 'Heavenly Father'.

Speaking at the Roman seminary he had himself attended fifty years earlier, he talked about how the

Vatican officials would talk about him in the third person. '"The pope should be told this", or, "This is a matter for the pope". And I would think of the Holy Father Pope Pius, whom I loved and venerated, and suddenly I would realise, they were talking about me!'

JOHN PAUL II:
Return to Poland

When a new pope is elected and agrees to take on the burden of office, there is no looking back. He cannot first nip home and say goodbye to his friends and family. Like the first disciples called by Jesus he must drop everything and start a new life in obedience to the call.

For Cardinal Wojtyla, a passionately patriotic Pole, and the first non-Italian to become pope in 450 years, he had to accept that he might never again return to the land of his birth. Never again walk on the mountains he loved. 'God has decreed that I remain in Rome,' he wrote to his cousin.

His election triggered immense jubilation in his home country, an outbreak of spontaneous celebration that the killjoy state could do nothing to curb. Pope John Paul telephoned home and asked, 'What is it like in Poland?'

'We are all weeping,' came the reply.

'Then come to Rome and we will all weep together.'

Old friends did manage to come to see him and when one knelt to kiss his ring, he gave him a gentle rebuke. 'Stand up, you must never bend your knee to me!'

It was not until the summer of 1979, eight months after taking office that he could make his first trip to Poland. There was no possibility of it being a simple matter of slipping home unnoticed. John Paul's return was an occasion for national celebration.

The Polish Communist government imposed restrictions on media coverage, but was powerless to prevent the capital city from being decked with flags and flowers. A 30-foot high wooden cross was erected in Warsaw's Victory Square and the Polish pope celebrated mass there in front of 300,000 people. When he was refused permission to visit the miners in Silesia, a quarter of a million miners, wives and family members came to him. He also paid a solemn visit to the death camp of Auschwitz, accompanied by former prisoners dressed in their striped camp uniforms. The pope knelt in prayer at the notorious Execution Wall.

The Eastern bloc leaders had been alarmed and infuriated by Pope John Paul's election. Inevitably there were tense, behind-the-scenes talks with government leaders for him to attend. The regime feared, correctly, that the visit might be the start of a process of political change. When the workers at the Lenin shipyard in

Gdansk went on strike a year later, they tied portraits of the pope and the Madonna to the perimeter fence.

John Paul also spent time in retreat at Jasna Gora, the site of the shrine to the Black Madonna, said to be the heart of the nation's spiritual life. Spiritually, emotionally and physically it was a tough and demanding return visit.

He did however find time for a convivial reunion with some of his old university friends. They kept him up until midnight singing the songs from their student days. One song had the line, 'May you live a hundred years!'

'Do you really want the pope to live that long?' John Paul asked.

'Yes, of course,' they said.

'Then you had better let him retire to bed and get some rest,' he replied with a chuckle.

JOHN XXIII:
Vatican Affairs

Angelo Roncalli, the peasant farmer's son, quickly had it confirmed to him as the newly elected Pope John XXIII that what he had long suspected was true. The Vatican was a hotbed of Machiavellian intrigue. It was not as corrupt a body as in the days of the Borgias, but there were certainly many officials who were more worldly than they were holy. No specific scandals came to light, as they were to do later in the affairs of the Vatican Bank, but there were undoubtedly many high-ranking clerics who lived well off considerable personal means. Some were the sons of wealthy highborn families with interests and influence in Italian politics and finance.

It would be wrong to suggest that the whole Italian Church was sunk in corruption, but it would be equally wrong to imagine that worldly temptation was unknown in the Vatican. The shrewd Pope John was well aware of what was happening.

The late Peter Hebblethwaite, the respected

observer of Vatican affairs and biographer of Pope John told a telling story; no names were mentioned, but the story came, he assured us, from an impeccable source.

A certain cardinal of aristocratic origins was on his deathbed. He had been engaged in the financial operations of the Vatican for many years. Pope John was worried that the aged cardinal might die unshriven, his soul in agony as much as his body. He sent a friar to hear his last confession. The friar returned crest-fallen, and reported that the cardinal's relatives had refused to let him through to the bedroom to see the dying man.

'Just as I thought,' said Pope John angrily. 'Send an archbishop. The family won't refuse an archbishop.' But they did.

So the pope sent a cardinal who was able to pull rank, get access to the deathbed, hear his fellow cardinal's confession and pronounce absolution.

But why had the nephews and nieces made it so difficult? The pope had his suspicions. They did not want anyone from the Church to persuade their rich uncle to change his will.

'I was born poor,' Pope John wrote in his journal, 'and will be very happy to die poor.'

JOHN XXIII:
Pilgrimage

As the cardinals, bishops, theologians and observers set out on their journeys to Rome for the Second Vatican Council, some traveling thousands of miles to be there, Pope John XXIII embarked on a journey of his own. For the first time in over 90 years a pope went on pilgrimage. On 4 October 1962, exactly one week before the Council was due to convene, Pope John travelled by train to two of Italy's most popular pilgrimage destinations, Loreto and Assisi.

The purpose was to pray for the work of the Council. As he foresaw that its deliberations would herald change and modernisation, Pope John also wished to re-root himself in some of the much-loved traditions of the Church; to reconnect with the grassroots faith of his flock. It would be a signal of reassurance to them.

Loreto is the site of the Holy House, the home of Mary, where she was born and where she was visited by the Angel Gabriel to be told that she would be the mother of Jesus.

The house had originally been in Nazareth, but in the late thirteenth century, so legend tells, it was carried across the sea by angels from the Holy Land. When the villagers found it they were dumbfounded and confused. However Mary appeared to the local priest who told him, 'This house has come to your shores by the power of God, of whom nothing is impossible'.

Perhaps instinctively, the peasant pope, who had first visited the shrine 62 years earlier, appreciated that devotion and folk faith were every bit as important as scholarly discourse.

Pope John also went as a pilgrim to Assisi, famed for its associations with St Francis, whose life and example had been his personal inspiration since boyhood. If the Council was to stress the need for the Church to be there for the poor, St Francis should be its patron, Pope John said. There will only be peace in the world, he said in his Assisi sermon, if there is a fair distribution of wealth.

There was great media interest in the pope's journey. Senior political figures met or accompanied Pope John. It was a journey too of public reconciliation between the Italian state and the Holy See, healing rifts that had dated back to the previous century. Thousands of people came to see their pope and he was welcomed along the way by crowds at all the railway stations through which he passed.

At Loreto he said that his prayer for the Council was that it should be a joyful declaration of the Gospel, leading to greater harmony and justice in the world. Mary, he declared, would be its 'leading star'.

FRANCIS:
Mary, the Untier of Knots

In the Church of St Peter am Perlach in Augsburg in Germany there is an intriguing and, to many viewers, baffling painting.

Executed some three centuries ago by Johan Schmidtner in the then fashionable Baroque style, it shows the Virgin Mary accompanied by angels untying a knotted ribbon. At her feet is a knotted serpent. The picture symbolises how Mary's obedience to God unloosed the bonds of sin caused by Eve's disobedience. Devotion to 'Mary, the Untier of Knots', it is said, helps people with troubled minds sort out and redirect their lives.

The painting had a profound effect on Fr Jorge Bergoglio when in 1986 he came face to face with it. He was by then 50 years old and in Germany ostensibly to complete work on a doctorate. But more than that, he was in a kind of exile from his home country of Argentina. The difficult years of the Dirty War had taken their toll. The Church had lost much respect and many Argentinians were especially critical of Jorge Bergoglio, the leading Jesuit. His conscience was also troubled. Could he, should he, have done more? It was best he take time out to reflect.

When he eventually returned home, it was not to take up a senior position in Buenos Aires. He was sent to a Jesuit community 400 miles away where, in the words of his biographer Paul Vallely, he 'languished in penitential obscurity'.

Inspired by the painting, through Jesuit spiritual discipline and a thorough examination of his life so far, a much-changed Jorge Bergoglio emerged when, to his surprise, he was called in 1992 to be an assistant bishop.

Jesuits do not normally seek preferment in the Church and as a bishop Jorge Bergoglio's connection with the order loosened. Given the history it was a welcome move.

Slowly Bishop Bergoglio's image began to change. In 1998 he became archbishop. He took it upon himself to speak out on behalf of the disadvantaged and in one memorable sermon in his cathedral told President

Kirchner and assembled ministers some uncomfortable truths about their inequitable economic policies and political posturings. The president called him the spiritual head of the political opposition and refused to listen to any of the archbishop's sermons again.

As well as speaking out he was a man of example and action, regularly visiting slum parishes and choosing to live a simple lifestyle, preferring boarding a bus to being chauffeur driven.

President Kirchner's widow, Cristina, by then herself president was the first head of state to visit Pope Francis after his election. She was a realist and knew that his election had been hugely popular back home. Despite their past differences, the meeting was extremely friendly. She gave him a *mate* set, to make the Argentinian national drink. She was unsure whether Vatican protocol allowed her to touch the Holy Father. Pope Francis, however, thanked her for the gift and for her visit with a kiss.

JOHN PAUL II:
Bishop at the Vatican Council

Bishop Wojtyla was an active participant in the Second Vatican Council. He was roughly half the age of Pope John XXIII who had convened the great Church gathering and as he contributed to the debates the young Polish bishop was quickly noted to be an up-and-coming talent. One of the topics he proposed for discussion was that priests should have an active involvement in all areas of life, including theatre and sport. He also hoped the Council would consider the vexatious mystery of how God could have allowed Auschwitz and the Gulags to have happened.

As he left Poland for Rome he wrote, 'I set out on this road with the deepest emotion, with a tremor in my heart.'

At its conclusion he was keen to implement the key changes proposed, even though his superior, Cardinal Wyszynski, was of a different mind. He did not believe the Church was in need of major reform and disliked the new liturgies very much.

But at the outset the two Poles were of one mind in finding the Council a strange experience. So many bishops were speaking freely about all kinds of issues. They were even openly, and sometimes rudely, disagreeing with each other. In Poland the Church was used to keeping a discreet unity, given the difficult political climate in which it had to work.

Bishop Wojtyla's gift for languages proved immensely useful. It helped him converse with fellow bishops from around the world and learn from their experiences. His knowledge of Latin enabled him to participate in the plenary sessions, where the ancient language of the Church was used, in order, said some suspiciously, to allow the traditionalists in the Curia to keep control.

When John XXIII died, the work of the Council continued under Paul VI. Archbishop Wojtyla, who had been appointed to the Archbishopric of Cracow during the Council, attended all sessions and was involved in the important committee work that drafted the key recommendations and teachings.

He left a strong impression on many, especially the new pope, for his intellectual rigour and lucidity. Shortly afterwards Paul VI created him Cardinal Wojtyla.

Others recall a more human side to the man. One day it snowed heavily in Rome and the Polish archbishop walked to the Vatican through the drifts to begin work on one of the committees. He was spotted on arrival wringing out the wet snow from the base of his cassock and sitting by a stove in bare feet drying his socks, laughing and relaxed.

JOHN XXIII:
The Cuban Missile Crisis

In October 1962 the affairs of the Second Vatican Council, that had taken so much preparation and on which so many hopes rested, was overshadowed by a world crisis of potentially catastrophic importance. The Cuban Missile Crisis was the diplomatic stand-off between the US President Kennedy and the Russian Soviet leader Khrushchev that brought the world to the brink of nuclear war. Indeed the American evangelist Billy Graham spoke of the end of the world being imminent.

Discrete, behind-the-scenes requests had been made to the Vatican that the Pope might in some way be able to defuse the situation. John F. Kennedy was a Roman Catholic and the Russian leader was known to respect Pope John XXIII as he had welcomed the Cuban ambassador to the Holy See.

As international tension mounted the pope spent much time in prayer in his private chapel. On 24

October at his Wednesday public audience he added some extra words to his address to signal that the crisis was much on his mind and that peace was the only option.

He then sent a message to the Kremlin urging negotiation and on the Friday of that week broadcast on Vatican Radio. His words were heard by the official Russian news media and *Pravda* reported them under the headline 'We beg all leaders not to be deaf to the cries of humanity'.

On the Sunday the tension lifted. The ships carrying nuclear missiles from Russia to Cuba turned back. Pope John celebrated a mass in relief and gratitude.

President Kennedy wrote to thank the pope for the part he had played. Nikita Khrushchev publicly acknowledged the pope's contribution. Historians looking back at the period have concluded that the importance of the pope's intervention on behalf of the people of the world should not be underestimated. It allowed the Russian leadership to back down and at the same time save face.

Pope John XXIII began work on his encyclical *Pacem in Terris*, peace on Earth, in the shadow of the crisis.

In 1963 relations between Moscow and the Vatican improved through personal contacts. Rada Khrushchev, the daughter of the soviet leader, visited Rome with her husband and met the pope. They spoke in their common language of French and after the formalities the conversation became easy. It is reported that she told the pope, 'You have big and hard hands like the farmers, like those of my father'.

'Tell me the names of your children,' the Pope said. 'When a mother speaks the names of her children something special happens.'

'Nikita, Alexei and Ivan,' Rada replied.

'Ivan!' exclaimed the Pope. 'That of course means John, my father and grandfather's names and the one I chose to be known by. When you go home give all your children a hug from the pope, but a special one for Ivan.'

JOHN PAUL II:
Assassination Attempt

Just after Christmas in 1983 Pope John Paul travelled to Rome's Rebibbia Prison, but it was no ordinary pastoral visit. He went in particular to see the prison's most notorious inmate, a Turkish terrorist named Mehemet Ali Acga.

The pope asked to be left alone with Ali Acga in his cell. The two men had much to talk about. For half an hour, they could be seen through the grille in the cell door sitting closely together, the pope occasionally touching the prisoner on the arm or knee to emphasise his words. They spoke in Italian and although Vatican and prison officials tried hard to hear what was being said, the conversation was not overheard.

What can be surmised with certainty is that the pope offered Ali Acga words of forgiveness. But he also had a question to ask. 'Why did you try to kill me?'

It was the afternoon of Wednesday 13 May 1981 and the pope was surrounded by thousands of pilgrims in St Peter's Square. They cheered as his car moved slowly through the crowd. Sometimes he stopped to bless a child or clasp a hand.

Suddenly guns shots were heard!

There were at least three sharp cracks like fireworks. The pope collapsed. His security team leapt into action. The car accelerated. The crowd looked on in disbelief. An ambulance was called and the pope rushed to hospital.

On arrival, his blood pressure was alarmingly low and his pulse faint. John Paul was unconscious and in need of urgent surgery. As he was taken to the operating theatre the sacrament of extreme unction was given. Wounds to his hand and arm could be seen, but the true extent of his internal wounds was unknown. There was no way of telling if he would live or die.

The wounds in his abdomen were extensive and the bleeding heavy. The surgeons however found that none of the essential organs or blood vessels had been destroyed. The spinal nerves too were untouched. The pope would live.

Two pilgrims in the crowd were also hit by the would-be assassin's bullets. They too were taken to hospital. It was a miracle, noted the pope's security team later, that no one had been killed.

The man who fired the gun was quickly apprehended and taken into custody. The police identified him as a known terrorist suspect, Ali Acga.

Following surgery, it took the pope several months to recover his strength and he had time to ponder the events. He had been shot, he noted, on the Feast Day of Our Lady of Fatima. He asked to see the text of the hitherto unpublished third secret of Fatima. He discovered in it a prophecy, which he interpreted as foreseeing the attempt on his life. But how was he to understand his remarkable escape, that essential arteries and vital organs were, astonishingly undamaged?

'One hand fired the gun', the pope concluded, 'but Our Lady's hand guided the bullet.'

FRANCIS:
Living Simply

According to tradition, when the Church is between popes, the papal apartments on the top floor of the Apostolic Palace at The Vatican, are closed and sealed.

Twenty-four hours after his election the new Pope Francis was taken to his new quarters, the red ribbon on the heavy wooden doors was cut, and he was shown his new home.

With an entourage of Vatican officials in tow he toured the ten rooms of living and working space.

They were a far cry from the rooms Pope Benedict had inherited. The apartments under John Paul II were, in the words of one Polish visitor, gloomy. Some of the furniture would not have been out of place in an apartment in a drab Warsaw suburb!

Pope Benedict had had the apartments overhauled. The electrics were outdated and the water pipes were encrusted with rust and limescale. According to one report, workers discovered big drums above a false

73

ceiling placed there to catch the leaks from the roof. The pope's bedroom, was completely redecorated.

Pope Francis's first reaction on seeing the apartments was that they were far too big. He decided to stay on in Room 201 at the Vatican guest house of St Martha.

Moving into the Papal Apartments was one of several trappings of office he opted to do without. Sharp-eyed observers noticed his footwear. He was not wearing the traditional papal red slippers. He kept his own sturdy black shoes.

He traded in the papal Mercedes for a Ford Focus and shortly after his election took the bus with his fellow cardinals instead of riding in the official car.

One rumour has circulated that Francis sometimes sneaks out of the Vatican, dressed as a priest, to distribute alms to those living on the streets. He has certainly embraced new technology. Instead of writing formal letters couched in Vatican-speak, he telephones or sends emails, signed just 'Francis'.

Pope Francis is said to enjoy the family atmosphere of St Martha's. He likes the company of fellow priests, Vatican visitors and the guest house staff. Popes have been expected to eat alone, but on his 77th birthday in 2013, after celebrating mass, Pope Francis enjoyed a communal breakfast. He invited the household staff to join him, along with four of the homeless men from the streets outside. One of them even brought Bob Marley, his dog, for a papal blessing!

JOHN XXIII:
A New Relationship

Until the pontificate of Pope John XXIII, one of the prayers used in the traditional Catholic Good Friday liturgy included a reference to the 'perfidious', or faithless and treacherous Jews. The word was a hangover from a former age when the Church had taught explicitly, or by implication, that the Jewish people had been responsible for crucifying Jesus.

On hearing the word being used at a Vatican service, the new pope immediately instructed that it be removed.

The revised prayer for the Jewish people now petitioned 'Almighty and eternal God, who dost also not exclude from thy mercy the Jews' that he might 'remove the veil from their hearts; so that they too may acknowledge Jesus Christ our Lord'.

During the Second World War many Jews fleeing from persecution were very grateful to Archbishop Roncalli. Istanbul was on the escape route for Jews escaping from Nazi-occupied Europe. He helped Jews by using diplomatic couriers to send them baptismal certificates. He also arranged for visas to be sent, many of which were forged. He liaised with Jewish organizations and lobbied the Vatican to help Jewish families in danger, for instance by approaching neutral countries to ask that they offer temporary asylum to Jewish families. He requested, unsuccessfully, that Vatican Radio broadcast that helping Jews was an act of mercy approved by the Church.

Often he saw the Vatican's unhelpful response as one of frustrating and callous indifference. He could not say as much in public, but behind the scenes his actions spoke louder than words. Through his intervention thousands of Jews from Slovakia, who were in danger of being sent to the concentration camps, obtained visas to travel to Palestine.

His wartime humanitarian concern and work with, and on behalf of, Jewish refugees shaped his own attitudes to Church teaching. One of the legacies of his time as pope and of the Vatican Council was the publication in 1965 of a new statement of Catholic teaching. The passion of Christ 'cannot be charged against all the Jews, without distinction. The Jews should not be presented as rejected or accursed by God'.

When a Jewish delegation met with Pope John XXIII at the Vatican they sensed a distinct change in the Church's attitude. After centuries of official tension, the friendly and approachable pope greeted them with the words of reconciliation from the Old Testament spoken to Jacob's sons in Egypt: 'I am Joseph your brother.' It marked the beginning of a new relationship.

FRANCIS:
Following St Francis

On election as pope, Cardinal Bergoglio chose the name Francis. He was the first pope to do so and it was a name of great significance. He was naming himself after St Francis of Assisi.

St Francis lived 800 years ago and dedicated his life to reforming the Church of his day by teaching and example. At a time when many leaders and clergy of the Church of the day lived sumptuously, he deliberately chose a life of great simplicity. He has been remembered too for his love of nature, as the saint who reverenced all living creatures.

He was also a man who had undergone a major

change in his life as an adult, turning his back on privilege and wealth to identify with the poor. In choosing the name the new pope was making a statement that his would be a humble and reforming ministry.

The name Francis also brought to many people's minds St Francis Xavier, the co-founder of the Jesuit order to which the pope belongs, and the bishop and doctor of the Church, St Francis de Sales.

Explaining his choice of name Pope Francis described a moment during the papal election when he realised that he might soon find himself chosen. He was sitting with two friends, fellow cardinals, who offered him words of encouragement. When it finally became apparent that Jorge Bergoglio had secured two-thirds of the votes, and had been elected, one of the friends turned to him, gave him a hug of congratulations and said by way of advice, 'Don't forget the poor.'

'Right away, thinking of the poor, the name Francis of Assisi came to mind,' the pope later said. 'Then I thought of all the wars in the world and that Francis was a man of peace. That is how the name Francis came to my heart.'

In October 2013, Pope Francis visited Assisi, the saint's hometown. He took the opportunity to outline his vision for the future of the Church. He prayed that it might resemble St Francis's 'Church of the poor'. The Roman Catholic Church today should, in all humility, serve the poorest in society, Pope Francis said. It must strip itself of all 'vanity, arrogance and pride'.

JOHN PAUL II:
9/11

On 11 September 2001 Pope John Paul was resting at Castel Gandolfo, his summer retreat near Lake Albano, when news broke of the attack on New York's World Trade Center. The event, now universally known as 9/11, was broadcast live around the world and millions of people watched their televisions in horrified astonishment as airliners were deliberately flown into one of the city's most famous landmarks. Almost 3000 people lost their lives in the attacks.

Though in poor health, the 81-year-old pope knew immediately he had a two-fold duty: first to pray for peace; and secondly to offer spiritual comfort and consolation to a shocked Church and world.

He immediately went to his private chapel and became engrossed in prayer. Through Vatican channels he issued a statement expressing his horror at the 'inhuman terrorist attacks'. He sent a message to the American president, 'I hurry to express to you and your fellow citizens my profound sorrow and closeness in prayer.'

The next morning he was flown by helicopter back to Rome where he addressed the Wednesday morning crowds in St Peter's Square. Normally the pope is applauded by the faithful as he arrives, on this occasion the mood was quiet and respectful.

Behind the scenes Vatican officials were in a highly nervous state. They feared that the Vatican might be the next target for a high-profile Al-Qaeda strike. Whatever the risk, the pope sensed that his role was to be in Rome and to be seen.

He told his listeners, 'Yesterday was a dark day in the history of humanity, a terrible affront to human dignity. After receiving the news, I followed with intense concern the developing situation, with heartfelt prayers to the Lord. How is it possible to commit acts of such savage cruelty? The human heart has depths from which schemes of unheard-of ferocity sometimes emerge, capable of destroying in a moment the normal daily life of a people. But faith comes to our aid at these times when words seem to fail.'

The next day he met with James Nicholson, the newly-appointed American ambassador to the Holy See for the formal presentation of his diplomatic credentials. It had been planned as a festive occasion, the ambassador later recalled, 'instead, it was a sad event, as the world was grieving the horrific events of just 48 hours prior'.

This was an attack on all of humanity, not just the USA, the pope told the ambassador. 'We must stop these people who kill in the name of God.'

Words the ambassador understood to be the pope, not only offering prayer and condolence, but also lending his moral backing to America's planned response.

FRANCIS:
Calling Home

As the newly-elected pope, Francis left the Vatican on his first morning in office to visit Rome's oldest church, the Basilica of Santa Maria Maggiore where he prayed and laid flowers on the altar. On the return journey he called by at the hotel where he had been staying just before the conclave. He said he wished to pick up his luggage and proceeded to surprise his officials and the hotel staff by insisting on settling his outstanding bill.

Despite a hectic schedule of meetings, learning new protocols and getting to know the Vatican staff, he still found time for the small things of life.

Following the example of St Francis of Assisi, whose name he had taken, Pope Francis believed in the importance of simple courtesies.

He called his sister Maria Elena, his only surviving sibling and several old friends. He asked that they pray for him. He called his dentist to cancel an appointment. He ordered another pair of shoes, but not red ones, he stipulated. He astonished the owners of a Buenos Aires newspaper kiosk, by calling in person to cancel his order.

Luis Del Regno or his son Daniel used to deliver the day's newspapers to Cardinal Jorge's home. On Sundays, he would call by at the vending kiosk very early to collect his copy of *La Nación*. Once a month he returned a pile of rubber bands, the ones the news-vender had used to keep the papers from falling apart when he delivered them. Often on a Sunday the cardinal would stay a few minutes to chat before taking a bus to the suburb of Lugano where he had a regular appointment serving *mate* to young people and the sick.

The cardinal had also baptised Luis's grandson.

But when the phone rang and a voice said, 'It's Cardinal Jorge', it took Daniel a few moments to believe that he was not being hoaxed.

'Seriously, it's Jorge Bergoglio, I'm calling you from Rome,' the Pope insisted.

'I was in shock, I broke down in tears and didn't know what to say,' Daniel told the Argentinian press. 'He thanked me for delivering the paper all this time and sent best wishes to my family.

'I asked him if there would ever be the chance to see him here again. He said that for the time being that would be very difficult, but that he would always be with us.'

Perhaps Daniel had suspected that their cardinal might be elected as he had asked him before he left if he thought he might be chosen.

'That is too hot to touch. See you in 20 days, keep delivering the paper,' was the future pope's reply.

So Cardinal Bergoglio booked a return ticket from Buenos Aires to Rome. Just before he left, friends noticed that his shoes were so shabby they insisted on buying him a new pair for such an important journey.

JOHN PAUL II:
Visiting Canterbury

Pope John Paul's pastoral visit to Britain in 1982 was almost cancelled at the last moment. Despite months of careful planning and the eager anticipation of the country's six million Roman Catholics, barely eight weeks before the pope's plane was due to touch down, international events intervened. Argentina invaded the Falkland Islands, Britain sent a military taskforce to recapture them and the two countries were at war.

Pope John Paul was faced with a delicate diplomatic problem. Thousands of miles away in the South Atlantic there were men, for whom he had ultimate spiritual responsibility, who were fighting and killing each other.

In the event the visit proceeded, but almost immediately afterwards the pope also flew to Argentina. The war was at its height during his time in Britain. News bulletins divided their air time between reports of his progress and his papal message urging peace, and dispatches from the war-zone giving details of casualties.

By the time John Paul reached Buenos Aires the fighting was over and his role was to console the bereaved and help heal the wounded pride of a nation.

One of the highlights of the pope's visit to England was his meeting with the Archbishop of Canterbury. Canterbury, said the pope, reminded him of Cracow. The two Church leaders knelt side by side in prayer on the spot where St Thomas Becket had been martyred. After the formal meeting, and as the pope was following a demanding schedule, Archbishop Runcie suggested he take a short rest. 'When in Canterbury,' John Paul agreed, 'the pope does what the archbishop tells him.'

Everywhere Pope John Paul went he received an enthusiastic welcome. Hundreds of thousands attended open air masses. There were however a few dissidents. The umbrella sellers, who had invested in thousands of white and yellow brollies were disappointed that the weather remained unusually dry. And the fierce Protestant preacher Dr Ian Paisley, who a few years later was to denounce Pope John Paul as the anti-Christ as he addressed the European Parliament, travelled the country staging street protests.

In Liverpool he stood on a street corner with his followers. Earlier he had told them in a fiery sermon that anyone blessed by the pope was cursed by God.

As the pope passed by, he turned to them with a mischievous twinkle in his eye, and raised his hand in blessing.

FRANCIS:
The Disfigured Man

For all his adult life, Vinicio Riva has felt as if he were a social outcaste. As a child he had been diagnosed with a rare genetic condition, neurofibromatosis. By the time Vinicio was a teenager the painful tumours growing on his body had become conspicuous and disfiguring. Unsightly lumps covered his head and face. Wherever he went he attracted stares, comments and even gasps of horror. People avoided him fearing they might catch some dreadful disease. Even Vinicio's father became too embarrassed to hug his son.

The doctors did not expect him to live much past 30 years of age.

But Vinicio defied the doctor's predictions and at the age of 53 decided to visit Rome and see the new Pope Francis. On the first Wednesday of November he joined the crowds in St Peter's Square to receive the communal blessing. The trip was the idea of a friend with whom Vinicio had previously travelled on pilgrimage to Lourdes.

In the square, Vinicio stood with others who had illnesses or disabilities. Towards the end of the pubic audience the new pope approached them. On seeing Vinicio, Francis immediately went up to him. As Vinicio formally kissed the pope's hand, Francis, with his other hand began caressing Vinicio's head and wounds. 'Then he drew me to him in a strong embrace,' Vinicio recalled.

The disfigured man placed his enlarged, tumour-covered head on the pope's chest. The pope, kissed him gently, stroked him and then laid his own head against Vinicio's. For what, to Vinicio, seemed like an age they remained together, wordless as Vinicio absorbed the healing comfort of touch.

'Sometimes you can say more when you say nothing,' Vinicio said later trying to describe the moment. 'I'm not contagious, but Pope Francis didn't know that. He caressed my whole face and while he was doing it, I felt only love.

'I tried to speak, to say something but I was unable to. The emotion was too strong. It lasted a little longer than a minute but it felt as if it were eternity. It was as if I had arrived in Paradise.'

The encounter was captured in a photograph. The image of the pope and Vinicio was seen around the world. In a reference to the film, some of the popular press insensitively captioned the picture, 'The Pope and the Elephant Man'.

Others however recalled another Francis from a former age, St Francis of Assisi, and the story of how he would visit the homes of lepers, not only to distribute alms, but also to touch, hug and kiss them with love and compassion.

JOHN PAUL II:
Sister Kane

Pope John Paul II broke with many of the traditions of the Church. He became the world's most travelled pope and declared more saints than any other pope before him.

Yet for all this, in many ways he was extremely conservative in his opinions. He had supported the liturgical changes brought about by the Vatican Council of Pope John XXIII, but steadfastly upheld traditional teaching on morality, contraception and abortion.

On the issue of priests being allowed to marry and that of women being ordained to the priesthood, he was also unmovable.

It was on his visit to the USA that he came face to face with the more radical wing of his Church. At the National Shrine of the Immaculate Conception in Washington, DC on 7 October 1979 the president of the Leadership Conference of Women Religious was due to give an address of welcome.

To begin with, the pope noted that Sister Theresa Kane was dressed, not in a habit, but a suit. He was not approving.

'Your Holiness,' she said, 'I urge you to be mindful of the intense suffering and pain which is part of the life of many women in these United States. I call upon you to listen with compassion and to hear the call of women who comprise half of humankind.

'As women we have heard the powerful messages of our Church addressing the dignity and reverence for all persons. As women we have pondered upon these words. Our contemplation leads us to state that the Church in its struggle to be faithful to its call for reverence and dignity for all persons must respond by providing the possibility of women as persons being included in all ministries of our Church.'

It was a direct call for the Church to reconsider its attitude towards the ordination of women to the priesthood. Pope John Paul was not expecting, and certainly not used to, such a direct and passionate call for a major change in Church custom and policy; and certainly not from a woman!

When it was his time to address the assembly, he did not respond to Sister Kane directly. One commentator said that he feigned not to have fully understood. He proceeded to give an address on the subject of the religious vocation. An indirect reference to Sister Kane might be inferred from his mention of the role of Mary, who mourned at the foot of the cross but was not present at the Last Supper.

Pope John Paul never changed his mind or attitude towards the role of women in the Church. Sister Kane has continued to promote her view.

That she left a lasting impression on John Paul is confirmed by a story told about a meeting 19 years later. Another member of her order had a meeting with the Pope and he asked if the sister knew Sister Kane.

When she replied that she did, John Paul asked, not once, but twice that she send her his regards.

FRANCIS:
Gestures of Reconciliation

Flying home from his papal visit to Brazil, Pope Francis held an impromptu press conference. He came to the cabin on the Alitalia plane where the journalists were seated and fielded a range of questions. The answer that created the headlines was on the subject of homosexuality. Without deviating from Church teaching on the subject, his tone was very different from that adopted previously by Church leaders.

'We must be brothers,' he said. 'If a person is gay and seeks God and has goodwill, who am I to judge him?'

The impact made by that simple response was considerable. It was the tone, not the words, that were to resonate. *The Advocate*, America's long-established gay rights magazine, even named Pope Francis as the 'single most influential person of 2013' on the lives of its readers.

Pope Francis has a long track record in reaching

out to those outside his Church, in a way that shows a real desire to connect, without compromising his principles. Sometimes simple gestures have been more powerful than words.

In Holy Week 2001, as a newly-appointed cardinal, he was visiting a hospital in Buenos Aires when, in an impromptu gesture, he asked for a jug of water and proceeded to wash and embrace the feet of twelve AIDS patients. On another occasion he washed the feet of a group of young drug addicts, just as Christ had washed the feet of his disciples. As pope he continued the tradition and on a visit to a youth prison on Maundy Thursday 2013 he washed the feet of inmates, including those of two women and two Muslim prisoners.

His gestures of reconciliation have included not just those marginalised by society, but also those marginalised by the Church.

Bishop Jeronimo Podesta was an activist whose views and deeds had led him into conflict with the Vatican. He was a radical proponent of Liberation Theology. When he began a relationship with, and later married, his secretary, it gave the hierarchy the excuse to dismiss him. By 2000 he was living in poverty and dying. Archbishop Bergoglio was the only senior member of the Church to visit him and he administered the last rites as he approached death. For him pastoral considerations took precedence over Church politics.

He remained in contact with Clelia Luro, Podesta's

widow, until her death in 2013, even though she was well known as a political radical and a strong opponent of the rules of priestly celibacy. An unlikely friendship developed and she would talk to Cardinal Bergoglio regularly on the telephone. She was one of the people Pope Francis telephoned from the Vatican after his election.

'He is a man of gestures,' Clelia Luro once said, 'and some believe because of these gestures.'

JOHN PAUL II:
A Papal Wit

When John XXIII talked of letting the fresh air in to blow through the Vatican he was not only thinking of the changes in the Church that might be authorised by the Vatican Council he had convened. He was also talking about his own style. Never forgetting the humble origins of Angelo Roncalli, he found some of the stiff protocol of the papal court rather difficult to remember. If he forgot to refer to himself as 'we' instead of 'I', as was the tradition, he would joke to his officials, 'be patient, I am still practicing at being pope.'

Once he was asked how many people worked at the Vatican, and Pope John couldn't refrain from giving a mischievous reply. 'Oh, about half of them, I'd say.'

There is a story too told of his meeting, when he was Nuncio in Paris, with a very distinguished local rabbi. The two approached a narrow door together and both, in polite deference, paused to let the other through first. 'I think it's Old Testament before New

Testament, don't you?' said the pope with a smile.

It was when he was working in Paris that he invited his four brothers to stay. They were dressing in their best clothes before going out to see fashionable Paris life. None of them, it transpired, could knot a neck-tie. 'We don't wear them very often,' they explained, 'and when we do our wives tie them for us.'

'I can't tie one either and I don't have a wife. Which I suppose is why priests dress like this,' the nuncio said pointing to his clerical collar. The brothers decided to dispense with the formalities of dress.

And is this story true or apocryphal? That it is attached to John XXIII suggests something about the pope's character and humanity. In his time as a papal representative he was well known for being able to defuse a difficult situation with his gentle wit and issue a rebuke, if necessary, in the same style.

He was paying a visit to a convent of nuns dedicated to The Holy Spirit. He was met by the Mother. 'I'm the Superior of the Holy Spirit,' she said introducing herself.

'Then you are more important than me,' said the pope. 'I'm merely the Vicar of Jesus Christ on Earth.'

FRANCIS:
Number One Fan

As a boy the young Jorge would be taken by his father to watch football. The local team in Almagro was San Lorenzo and the future pope became a lifelong supporter.

As an adult he would regularly attend home matches and even when his duties as archbishop and cardinal were at their most demanding, he would make a point of interrupting work to watch his team on television or listen to radio commentaries of games.

In his room at the cardinal's house, amongst his many personal mementos, was a poster signed by the San Lorenzo squad. In 2011 he celebrated a mass for the team and was photographed with his footballing heroes.

The team had started as a youth project. Following an accident in which a boy had been killed by a tram when playing football in the street, a local priest, Lorenzo Massa, offered the boys space to play on some open ground near his Church, on the condition they would attend mass on Sundays. From those small beginnings the professional team grew.

In 2013, on hearing of their cardinal's election as pope, the team took to the field in a new strip – one showing a portrait of the new Pope Francis.

It was a memorable year for the team. In December several officials and players visited Pope Francis in Rome and presented him with a replica of the league trophy they had won and one of the gloves worn by their goalkeeper during the decisive match. He was also given a team jersey on which the words *'Francisco Campeon'* (Champion Francis) were displayed

After attending the pope's weekly audience in St. Peter's Square, the team representatives had their own extended meeting with the pope during which they discussed the crucial match that clinched the Torneo Inicial championship against local rivals Velez Sarsfield.

Pope Francis told them that he would be keeping the trophy and the glove in 'a Vatican museum'.

He presented the team with an icon of the Madonna, which the players said they would keep at their stadium to remind them of their 'number one fan'.

JOHN XXIII:
This Bed is my Altar

Pope John XXIII knew that his pontificate would not be a long one. He was an old man when elected to the office and soon after setting his plans in motion for the future of the Church, he was diagnosed with cancer.

Much of what he started he knew he would never see accomplished.

He celebrated his final Easter seven weeks before he died. 'The Easter message is full of light, not death but life, not conflict but peace, not lies but truth,' he told the congregation in St Peter's.

In his final months he was often weakened by

severe abdominal pain. Even when robing for mass he winced with pain at the effort. 'I'm like St Lawrence on the grid iron,' he joked.

He said his last mass on 17 May and realised at the time that he would probably never have sufficient stamina again to stand at the altar. On doctor's orders and because he could do no other, he took to his bed for longer and longer periods.

On Ascension Day, as he lay in bed, Pope John said to his night-nurse, Brother Frederico, that he wished he could say mass again. 'But this bed is your altar,' the brother replied.

'You are right,' said the pope. 'This bed is an altar, an altar needs a victim, and I am ready.'

As the end approached the papal sacristan anointed the pope. 'I had the great grace to be born into a Christian family, modest and poor, but with the fear of the Lord,' Pope John told him. 'My time on earth is drawing to a close. But Christ lives on and continues his work in the Church. Souls, souls, *Ut omnes unum sint*.' (That they all may be one.) The sacristan was so overwhelmed with emotion that he anointed the pope's senses in the wrong order and, drawing on his almost 60 years of pastoral experience, John XXIII guided him.

Pope John died on the morning of 3 June 1963. His last reported words, uttered twice over a few hours before his last breath, were those of St Peter.

'Lord, you know that I love you.'

JOHN PAUL II:
The Miracle of Sister Marie Simon-Pierre

As a young man Karol Wojtyła was a keen sportsman and when he became Pope John Paul II he was still a fit man who enjoyed exercise, especially hiking in the mountains.

The years in office however took their toll. He never fully recovered his strength after the assassination attempt and as the years went by old age inevitably caught up. In his final years Parkinson's Disease was diagnosed. Towards the end of his life both walking and talking were difficult.

Like many of his flock around the world, Sister Marie Simon-Pierre, watched his physical decline with sadness, but also some personal anxiety. The French maternity hospital nurse was barely 40 years of age, but she too had Parkinson's Disease. Her muscular control and energy were steadily declining. Watching the pope on television she said was very difficult, 'because I was thinking of how

I would face that same situation in the coming years'.

John Paul died on 2 April 2005 and only six weeks later the new pope, Benedict XVI, announced the beginning of the process that would lead towards the beatification of his predecessor.

Sister Marie Simon-Pierre's condition meanwhile had declined sharply. She had been forced to stop work. In their prayers, fellow members of the Little Sisters of Catholic Motherhood decided to ask John Paul to intercede. At her superior's suggestion, Sister Marie wrote the late pope's name down on a piece of paper, even though her hand was so unsteady, the writing was quite illegible.

When Sister Marie went to bed on the night of 2 June, everything was a struggle. Yet she work early the next day and was astonished at how different she felt.

'When I went to the chapel to pray, I realised that my arm was moving and it wasn't motionless beside my body. During the Mass I knew for certain that I had been cured.'

When her doctors examined her they confirmed that her symptoms had gone, but had no medical explanation. 'It's like a second birth,' she said. 'I feel like I've discovered a new body, new limbs.'

Since Pope John Paul II's death there have been many claims of miraculous cures. Sister Marie's case was carefully and methodically examined and declared authentic. It was the miracle cited when the Blessed John Paul was beatified on 1 May 2011.

JOHN XXIII:
The Miracle of Pope John

The sisters of the Congregation of the Daughters of Charity are an order of nuns who dedicate their lives to serving the least fortunate in society. One of their modern number, Sister Caterina Capitani, has followed her vocation as a hospital nurse. The sister, who is from Cosenza in Italy, has been described as a human dynamo; such has been her unflagging enthusiasm and willingness to work long hours.

The doctors she meets, and who know her story, have been amazed at her energy. Sister Caterina is a walking medical miracle. She has just the remnants of a stomach, no pancreas and no spleen. Instead of following a cautious lifestyle, resting often and eating very carefully, she has frequently pushed herself to limits most normal people would find exhausting.

In 1966 Sister Caterina began experiencing severe chest pains. One night she found her mouth full of blood. She told no one, fearing she might have to stop the nursing work she felt called to do.

Seven months later, she had a far more serious hemorrhage. She had no option but to seek medical advice. After lengthy investigations she underwent surgery. Ulcerous tumours were found inside and most of her stomach had to be cut away. They were caused, thought the doctors, by problems originating in the pancreas and spleen. They too were removed.

The next day, she offered a prayer of thanks to Our Lady, for having come through the operation safely. A fellow sister gave her a picture of the late Pope, John XXIII and suggested she pray to him as well.

Over the coming weeks Sister Caterina had many setbacks and remained seriously ill. The continuing problems came to a head when a hole opened in her abdomen. It started to leak blood and gastric acid.

She was brought a relic of Pope John to comfort her - a piece of the sheet upon which the Pope had died. It was placed on the open wound. Sister Caterina was certain she would die. As she lay waiting for the end, she became aware of a hand pressing the wound and the voice of a man calling her name. She turned towards the voice and saw Pope John standing by her bed. 'You prayed to me very much,' Pope John said, 'don't be afraid now ... you will be healed.'

The vision faded and after several minutes, Sister Caterina called her sisters. She asked for something to eat and when she had finished a small bowl of semolina, she said she was still hungry and asked for a full meal.

The doctors who examined her found no traces of illness. The healed wound had not even left a scar. Before long Sister Caterina returned to work, but not before she kept a promise she had made to Pope John. She wrote a full account of her experience, complete with the medical details. 'It may be needed one day,' the saintly pope had said.

JOHN PAUL II:
A Miracle in Costa Rica

History's most widely-travelled pope, John Paul II, touched down in Costa Rica in March 1983 on a whirlwind tour of Central America.

It was a hugely memorable day for the country where 75% of the citizens are Roman Catholics.

Floribeth Mora Díaz is from the small town of Tres Rios. Back then she was a young woman and like everyone excited by the first papal visit to their small country. Hundreds travelled from her community to catch a glimpse of him as he passed by in the bullet-proof popemobile.

Twenty-eight years later and that day was just a distant memory. Mora was now a mother of four children. She was suffering from severe, persistent headaches and hospital tests were needed to pin down the cause.

In due course, she was given some devastating news. The doctors had found an aneurysm in the brain, a weak spot in a blood vessel causing it to bulge or balloon. Should it burst, the results can be fatal.

She returned home to face a worrying future. 'I was terribly frightened of leaving my children,' she said. 'I was very scared of my illness but I always kept my faith. I have always been a firm believer, and I have a deep love of God.'

Like many devout Catholics in her country Mora had a small shrine at home where she would go to pray. It was decorated with flowers; there were candles to light, a crucifix and a rosary. Mora kept a picture there of Pope John Paul II, who she called 'my saint'.

On 1 May 2011, she was reminded of the joy of the pope's visit to her country as she watched television pictures from Rome of John Paul's beatification. So she prayed to him for strength.

As she prayed she believes she heard the voice of John Paul II speaking to her, telling her, 'Arise, do not be afraid.'

Afterwards, she surprised her husband by saying, 'I feel better', and from that moment her condition rapidly improved. Within six months hospital tests confirmed there was no indication in her brain that she had ever had an aneurysm. Alejandro Vargas Román, her neurosurgeon was convinced that her recovery was the result of divine intervention. 'I am a Catholic, and as a doctor with many years of experience I do believe in miracles. No one has been able to provide a medical explanation for what happened.'

Two years later Mora travelled with her husband to the Basilica of Our Lady of Guadalupe in Mexico. There during mass she told her remarkable story. It was 22 October, the feast day of Blessed John Paul II.

BIBLIOGRAPHY
and suggestions for further reading

Pray for Me: The Life and Spiritual Vision of Pope Francis, Robert Moynihan (Rider Books, 2013)

Man from a Far Country, Mary Craig (Hodder and Stoughton, 1979)

Living Peter, Glorney Bolton (George Allen and Unwin, 1961)

Pope John Paul II: In His Own Words, Anthony Chiffolo (ed.) (Random House, 1998)

The Pope in Winter, John Cornwell (Penguin, 2004)

Universal Father, Garry O'Connor (Bloomsbury, 2005)

John XXIII: Pope of the Century, Peter Hebblethwaite (Continuum, 2005)

A Call to Service: The Inside Story of Pope Francis, Stefan Von Kempis and Philip Lawler (SPCK, 2013)

Pope Francis: Untying the Knots, Paul Vallely (Bloomsbury, 2013)

Pope John XXIII: Essential Writings, Jean Maalouf (ed.) (Orbis, 2008)

Pope Francis, Matthew Bunson (Our Sunday Visitor, 2013)

Pope Francis: In His Own Words, Julie Schwietert Collazo and Lisa Rogak (William Collins, 2013)

On Heaven and Earth - Pope Francis on Faith, Family and the Church in the Twenty-First Century, Jorge Mario Bergoglio and Abraham Skorka (Bloomsbury Continuum, 2013)

Pope John Paul II: A Biography, Tad Szulc (Pocket Books, 1995)